FUN FAX™
SHARK

Written by Richard Addison
Illustrated by Stephen McLean
and Adam Young

MEET THE SHARK

How long have sharks been around?
A very long time. Sharks were swimming in the sea about 350 million years before man appeared and 200 million years before the first dinosaurs appeared!

Are all sharks big, sleek, grey killers?
No! In the first place, not all sharks are big. About half the 350 shark species are less than 1 metre long. The Lantern Shark could easily fit on your hand! Although there <u>are</u> big sharks - the Whale Shark is bigger than a truck!

All shapes and colours
Sharks like the Blue Shark are sleek and streamlined but some sharks have flat bodies (such as the Angel sharks), the Horn sharks have blunt heads and the Frilled Shark looks like a snake!

And not all sharks are grey. There are brown, blue, striped and spotted sharks, their skin often used as camouflage.

But are they all killers?
No! Some people are terrified of sharks but they are not all man-eating monsters! Only about 10% of shark species are thought to be dangerous to people. And amazingly, the two biggest sharks, the Whale and Basking sharks, are totally harmless!

Where do sharks live?

In all the world's seas and oceans, from very cold Arctic waters to the warm seas off Australia and Africa. Most sharks live far out to sea and some in very deep water. Some sharks live near the surface, some on the seabed.

Many like coastal waters and some are even found far up rivers and into lakes.

Not a bone in their body!

Instead, sharks have a skeleton made from some cartilage, which is softer and lighter than bone but tougher and more flexible. Cartilage feels a bit rubbery and is like the tissue found in your ears and at the tip of your nose!

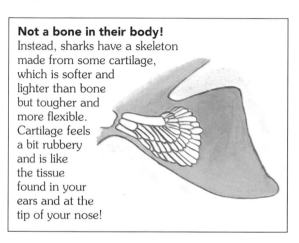

Do sharks have scales like other fish?

No. Sharks have very tough skin which is covered in tiny teeth called denticles. The skin feels rough like sandpaper. If a shark rubs against a swimmer, the skin alone can cause a nasty injury.

You might think that smooth skin would be best for slipping through water but rough skin actually works better. Scientists have even studied shark skin to try to copy it for submarine and aircraft design!

Is it true that sharks always have to keep moving?

In some cases, yes, because many sharks have to swim to breathe! As they move forward, sea water flows into the mouth and over special slits called gills in the throat which remove oxygen from the water.

If a shark stops swimming (for example, if it gets caught in a net), the shark can't breathe and could die. So sharks like the Great White and Mako have to swim non-stop during their whole life to stay alive!

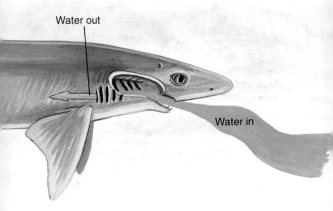

Water out

Water in

But some sharks live on the sea-bed and lie motionless. How do they breathe?

Easy. Sharks like Angel and Horn sharks have special muscles to pump water over the gills without having to swim forward.

SWIMMING, TAILS AND FINS

Sink or swim?

There is another reason why some sharks don't stop swimming.

Despite their light cartilage skeleton, sharks don't float well - in fact they are heavier than water! Unlike most fish, sharks don't have an adjustable balloon-like bag of air in their body. Fish use these bags (called swim-bladders) to move up and down in the ocean, but without this, sharks must either swim or sink!

Surely that's a bad thing for the shark?

Not really. By not having a swim-bladder, sharks can swim quickly and easily to different depths without having to wait for the bladder to empty or fill with air!

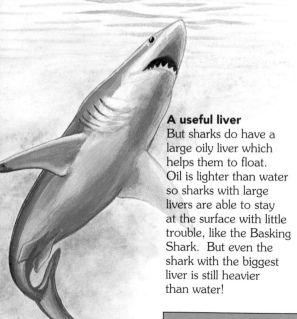

A useful liver

But sharks do have a large oily liver which helps them to float. Oil is lighter than water so sharks with large livers are able to stay at the surface with little trouble, like the Basking Shark. But even the shark with the biggest liver is still heavier than water!

Fast sharks

Most open ocean species cruise slowly at about 5 kph, beating their tails gently from side to side. They swim with very little effort and produce no bubbles or ripples, which is handy for sneaking up on prey! But sharks can swim very fast for short bursts up to 40 kph - but tire quickly at this speed and soon have to slow down to regain energy.

The glider and the jet fighter

The Blue Shark is often compared with a glider plane because of its very slim, sleek body. Its pectoral fins act like wings to keep it level in the water.

But the Great White and Mako sharks are shaped like jet fighters! They have muscular bodies and shorter pectoral fins like jet wings. Their crescent-shaped tail has a powerful thrust for fast acceleration.

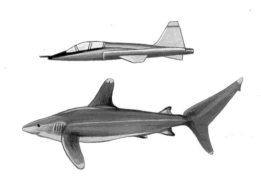

More aeroplanes

Unlike the fins of other fish which tend to be rather delicate, shark fins are large, thick flaps of skin. They are used for balance and to steer.

The pectoral fins are used to lift the shark in the water or when tilted, like brakes - just like the flaps of an aeroplane wing when landing!

These pectoral fins are even shaped like aeroplane wings. The leading (front) edge is rounded, but the rear edge is thin. This allows water to flow easily over them.

Walking fins!

Sharks that spend their lives on the sea-bed (like the Horn sharks) have soft, rounded fins and move slowly. They even use their pectoral fins to 'walk' along the bottom!

TEETH AND FOOD

Teeth - the shark's most famous feature

The teeth of the Great White Shark are the hardest substance that comes from any animal - their teeth are about as strong as stainless steel! It uses them in a bite which is 300 times stronger than yours!

Who needs a dentist?

Sharks don't, because they always have a good set! Most sharks have rows and rows of razor-sharp teeth. The first two rows are used for biting and behind these are between 5 and 15 rows of teeth folded flat, ready to move forward to replace any teeth that are lost, damaged or worn out.
So sharks never run out of teeth!

How fast can sharks replace their teeth?

Sometimes within a day! This is just as well because many teeth can be lost each time a shark launches an attack on a good sized victim, like a seal. Sometimes when a shark has attacked a person, their teeth have been found embedded in the person's skin!

A Lemon Shark can replace 30 teeth every week and Spiny Dogfish and Cookie-Cutters replace a whole row at a time.

During its life, a shark might get through 20,000 teeth! Different sharks have different teeth and experts can sometimes tell the species from just looking at a single tooth.

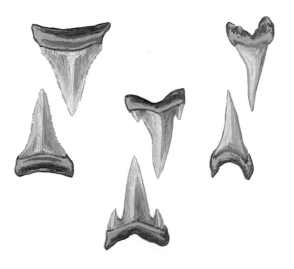

Sharks can dislocate their jaw

They do this to push the mouth (and all those teeth!) far forward past the overhanging snout to bite into their food. Once the prey is gripped, the jaw returns to its normal position. And all this happens within the blink of an eye!

The shape of the jaw allows the shark to have massive, powerful jaw muscles - so once in the mouth, there is little chance of anything escaping!

Razor-sharp

The Great White Shark has the biggest and sharpest teeth - they are triangular with jagged edges so they can easily slice through large fish, sea turtles, sea-lions, dolphins, even other sharks! A Great White tooth can be 3 inches long and its bite 30 inches wide! Great Whites will often take a bite out of their victim and wait for it to bleed to death or weaken before completing the meal!

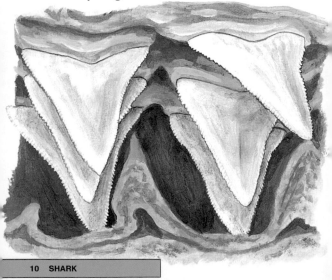

More nasty teeth

The teeth of the Tiger Shark are pointed and sharp with saw-like edges to 'saw' through their victim's flesh and bone, often while shaking their head violently from side to side.

The dustbin of the sea

Like many sharks, Tiger Sharks will eat virtually anything. All the following items have been found in shark stomachs: tin cans, car number plates, shoes, paint, coal, cushions, clothes, car tyres, bits of wood, a bottle of wine and even bits of dead chickens and cows that must have washed into the sea. A sheep's head was found in one shark and a dog in another! Even a porcupine has been found in a shark! And human legs and arms. Tiger Sharks even eat poisonous sea-snakes and jellyfish.

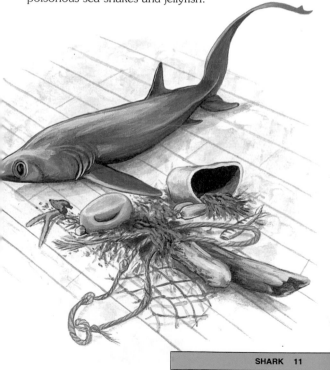

Crushing and grinding

Not all sharks need large sharp teeth. The Port Jackson Shark has strong, flat back teeth for crushing and grinding sea-urchins and crabs. And the Whale and Basking sharks feed on tiny plants and animals which they filter from the sea - they don't even need teeth!

How often do sharks eat?

This varies. Mako Sharks seem to like a meal every day but Great Whites sometimes go weeks without food. But when they do eat they make sure it's an enormous meal like a seal. And Basking Sharks may go the entire winter without food! Sharks that live in cold, deep oceans don't seem to need as much food.

Feeding frenzy!

Sharks spend much of their lives hunting alone for food. But sometimes two or more sharks will go for the same food. Other sharks soon join them, attracted by the blood and commotion and very soon a 'feeding frenzy' begins with over-excited sharks fighting each other for the food. Sometimes the sharks bite out at anything nearby, occasionally tearing each other apart!

**To find their food, sharks use the same
5 senses that you have - hearing, smell, sight,
taste and touch plus a sixth sense which you
don't have!**

1 Do sharks have ears?
Yes, they have very
sensitive internal ears
but no flaps of skin on
the outside as you do.

Ear hole

2 Nosey nostrils!
The sense of smell is very important to sharks.
They usually find food by smelling it first. Sharks can

smell blood from over a
kilometre away and detect
one drop of blood mixed
with millions of litres of
sea water.

3 Can sharks see well?
Fairly well. They can see up to about 20 metres
away but this is probably enough - sharks really
only use their eyes as they launch an attack, to see
movement rather than the shape of their prey.

Sharks can see in the dark!
If you were down in the murky depths of the
ocean you would find it hard to see anything.
But not a shark. A layer of cells in the back of
their eyes allow them to see in near darkness.

4 Do sharks taste their food?

Sharks do have taste buds in their mouths and will spit out food they don't like! Some scientists think sharks are also able to taste through cells in their skin - which is why sharks often 'bump' into their victim before they attack!

5 Touch - the lateral line

Sharks have a very sensitive line of cells under the skin running down each side of their body. This line feels the movements of any sea creatures nearby, particularly if the animal is injured or struggling. By following these vibrations, the shark can find the animal and eat it.
This sense is called 'distant-touch'.
Sharks may also feel pain and temperature changes.

Red shows the lateral line

6 The sixth shark sense

The Ampullae of Loreziniare are the tiny holes on the head and snout of sharks which can detect very weak electrical signals made by fish. This means that a shark can pinpoint a fish at night or in murky water and so hunt whenever it wants!

There's no hiding!

Using this sixth sense, sharks can even find fish hiding under the sand! As a shark swims over the sea-bed, the fish will still give out the electrical signals and be discovered.

FELLOW TRAVELLERS

Even when sharks are hunting alone, they are not really alone. They have smaller fish for company.

Pilot fish - fish which don't pilot!
It was once thought that pilot fish helped sharks to find food by 'piloting' them through the ocean. But really pilot fish just like swimming with sharks! There are two reasons for this - protection and free food. Pilot fish are protected from their enemies while they're with sharks and can also eat any scraps of food left by the shark!

The remora - the hitch-hiking fish!

The remora actually attaches itself to the shark's body for a free ride through the ocean. The remora has a strong sucker on top of its head enabling it to hold on for as long as it likes. No matter how fast the shark swims, the remora cannot be shaken off! Remoras can even slide backwards and forwards along the shark's body. Like pilot fish, remoras grab any bits of food left by the shark. Remoras are fast strong swimmers so this hitch-hiking is great laziness!

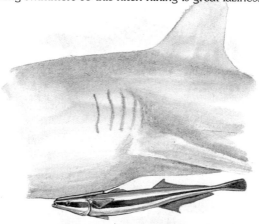

Shark parasites

Sharks are host to several types of parasite which dig in and feed off their skin and blood. Most aren't that harmful but they must surely irritate the shark.

Some sharks have hundreds of tapeworms, each about 30 centimetres long, living in their stomach!

Eye trouble

One type of parasite hangs onto the eye of the Greenland Shark, feeding on the eye surface! It can be very hard for the shark to see but the parasite doesn't let go!

BABY SHARKS

The numbers game

Most fish lay millions of eggs into the sea in the hope that just a few survive. These eggs are an easy target for other animals and most are eaten. But sharks are different. When born, the baby shark (called a pup) is well-developed and can swim and hunt for itself and has a good chance of surviving - it is like a smaller version of its parents. But there are dangers - shark pups have to spend much of their early life hiding from larger sharks which will attack and eat them!

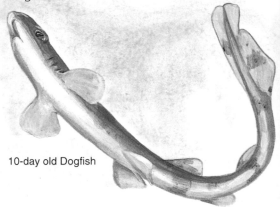

10-day old Dogfish

Love bites - the mating game

In order to mate two sharks first have to meet. This often means swimming a long way, sometimes to special breeding grounds if males and females live in different parts of the ocean.

When they meet, the male chases after the female, possibly attracted by her smell, and holds her fins with his teeth to keep her close! These love bites don't cut too deep and heal within a few weeks. Female Blue Sharks actually have thicker skins than the males to prevent injury while mating! Few people have seen sharks mating but some think they mate with their heads almost buried in the sea-bed!

Three ways to become a shark
Sharks grow and develop in 3 different ways before they are born. The first way is the most primitive and is called *oviparity*.

Egg case
Here the mother lays a few eggs on the sea-bed, protected in a tough, leather-like case. After about a month a tiny shark develops from the egg and begins to feed off the large yolk. After about seven months the shark has fins and can wriggle inside the egg case. Then after about a year, the baby shark chews out of the case and swims away. Small sharks that live on the sea-bed are often born this way, including the Port Jackson Shark. It lays eggs in bizarre corkscrew-shaped cases and wedges them in cracks in rocks for protection.

Baby shark hatching from egg

Egg of Port Jackson Shark

The mermaid's purse

These are the famous egg cases of Dogfish. About the size of your hand, empty purses are often washed up on beaches and look like they could be the purses of the mythical mermaid! Threads at the corners of the purse tangle on seaweed or coral to stop the eggs from being washed away before the shark hatches.

Whale of an egg!

Amazingly, the biggest shark of all, the Whale Shark, also lays eggs. These are enormous eggs, the biggest in the world at 30 centimetres. These are more like handbags than purses! But despite their size, Whale Shark eggs are very rarely seen.

Do sharks make good parents?

No! As soon as the baby sharks are born, the mother swims away to leave them to fend for themselves. A shark will sometimes even eat their babies!

The second way to become a shark - *ovoviviparity*.

This is the most popular method. This time the egg stays inside the mother while the shark grows.

Shark eat shark!

When all the yolk is gone, the strongest and most developed baby shark then starts to eat its brothers and sisters inside the mother's body! Often only one shark pup is left when the mother gives birth - even though there could have been 6-8 inside her at one stage.

Sharks that are born this way include Angel sharks, Basking, Mako and Sand Tiger sharks.

Shark giving birth to baby

The third way - the advanced way

Here, the baby shark doesn't feed from yolk in an egg but directly from the mother while it grows inside her. The baby shark could spend 9 months inside its mother - the same as a human baby! Blue, Bull and Hammerhead sharks are born this way - Hammerheads sometimes give birth to 40 young sharks at once!

THE WONDERFUL WORLD OF SHARKS

GREAT WHITE SHARK

The largest meat-eating fish At over 6 metres in length, the Great White or White Death is big enough to eat seals whole and even attack whales ...

... and people. Great Whites have made more attacks on people than any other species of shark.

Killer! The Great White is built for speed, power and to kill, with jaws that can bend steel bars and bite clean through a man's leg! Great Whites live in warm waters throughout the world, and are often found near sealion colonies which offer plenty of food!

Great Whites are often scared - their prey must sometimes fight back, or perhaps Great Whites fight each other! Unusually for a shark they will stick their head above the water during an attack.

BLUE SHARK

The long-distance swimmer Blue Sharks can swim vast distances very quickly. They are known to swim right across the Atlantic Ocean. One tagged Blue Shark had covered over 6,000 kilometres in 16 months. Another tagged off the south coast of England was caught near Brazil - that's 7,000 kilometres away.

Blue is beautiful

The Blue Shark is perhaps the most sleek, streamlined and beautiful shark, perfecting its shape over millions of years. It grows to about 5 metres and often cruises near the surface with its triangular-shaped dorsal fin sticking out of the water. Like the Great White, the colouring of the Blue Shark allows it to 'hide' in the ocean - its white underneath means it is hidden in the light above and the dark blue of its upper surface means it is hidden in the darker blue of the sea below.

TIGER SHARK
Fading stripes These fierce sharks grow to about 6 metres and often hunt in packs, sometimes moving into shallow waters to feed. Tiger Sharks are named after their tiger-like striped bodies. As they grow older, these stripes disappear!

BULL SHARK
A taste for fresh water This is one of the most dangerous sharks and at 3.5 metres it is certainly big enough to attack a person. Bull Sharks are often spotted near beaches and even swim up rivers and into freshwater lakes. One Bull Shark was seen 2,000 kilometres from the sea up the River Zambezi in Africa!

THRESHER SHARK

The shark with the incredible tail At 3 metres, the huge top lobe of the Thresher Shark's tail can be as long as its body! The tail is used to herd fish like mackerel or herring into a tight group before the Thresher swims through and eats them! Sometimes several Thresher Sharks will work together as a team.

Knock out! A Thresher Shark will also swim into a school of fish and lash its tail about like a whip, stunning or killing the fish. Anglers trying to catch a Thresher Shark are sometimes hurt by that enormous tail!

MAKO SHARK

The leaping shark This is an aggressive 4 metre shark with a nasty set of teeth to hold prey. It is also very fast, swimming at over 30 kph to catch tuna and swordfish. Makos often leap out of the water when trying to escape from anglers!

HAMMERHEAD SHARK

A head start The 5 metre long Hammerhead Shark is the only shark with that weird, flat, T-shaped head. This bizarre head may be useful for finding food. With eyes and nostrils at each end of the head, Hammerheads can see and smell very well, so if bait is put into the water to attract sharks, it is often a Hammerhead that appears first!

The food detector When searching for food, the Hammerhead swings its head from side to side to pick up the scent and the best direction to go. It also uses its head like a metal detector, picking up electrical signals from animals buried in the sea-bed!

The sting Hammerheads often eat Stingrays and don't seem to mind being stung by the tail. Perhaps they are immune to the sting. Hammerhead Sharks have been found with dozens of Stingray spines stuck in their throat and mouth!

Lots of hammers Sometimes hundreds of Hammerheads gather together and no-one knows why. Most of the sharks in these groups are females and they sometimes head-butt each other! Hammerheads are unpredictable sharks with several recorded attacks on people.

GREENLAND SHARK

The sleepy shark This is the only shark that lives its
whole life in cold Arctic waters. The Greenland
Shark reaches 8 metres and is sometimes called the
Sleeper Shark because of its lazy habits - it often
rests on the sea-bed. But it catches fish, seals, squid,
even diving sea-birds when cruising under the ice-
packs. Greenland Sharks have been known to attack
Eskimos in canoes, but usually they are sluggish and
harmless. In fact they are easily caught by Eskimos
who use hooks baited with bits of wood, but their
flesh is poisonous unless boiled many times.

Water surface

Ice

NURSE SHARKS

Scavengers! The slow swimming Nurse sharks are
related to the big Whale Shark and are found close
to shore, spending much of their time scavenging for
food on the sea-bed. Nurse sharks have a pair of
finger-like feelers called barbels on either side of their
head hanging down from their nose, which feel for
food in the sand.

Harmless?

Nurse sharks will attack if provoked. Sometimes
divers prod these sharks or pull their tails or even sit
on their backs while they lie on the sea-bed. Nurse
sharks are quite capable of biting off someone's
finger. And when they bite into something, they
tend not to let go!

SWELL SHARK

Double your size! Smaller than the Nurse sharks at about 1 metre, Swell Sharks can double their size if threatened by another animal. They gulp mouthfuls of water into their stomach and swell - this allows them to wedge between rocks! If a Swell Shark is lifted out of the water it can still swell - by gulping in air! The corners of the Swell Shark's mouth are folded like an accordion to allow for the stretching.

HORN SHARKS

Prehistoric looking! These 1.5 metre sharks are named after the 2 horn-like spines on their back. Horn sharks usually feed at night on shellfish from the sea-bed and rest during the day in underwater rock crevices. Like Nurse sharks, Horn sharks are sometimes annoyed by divers and will bite out!

Horn sharks often feed on purple sea-urchins which stain their teeth and spines purple!

Port Jackson Shark - pig or dog?

This Horn shark has been given two other names because of its looks! Some people call it the Pig Shark because its head and large nostrils make it look like a pig! Others think that its squashed up face and large ridges above the eyes make it look like a bulldog - hence the name Bulldog Shark.

WHALE SHARK

When is a whale not a whale? When it's a Whale Shark! This is the biggest fish and the biggest shark and is even as big as some whales. The Whale Shark can grow to 13-15 metres and weigh as much as a bus. Or three elephants. Or five rhinoceros. These are very fat sharks - it would take a tape measure 7 metres long to stretch around its body!

Thick skin The Whale Shark has thicker skin than any other animal (10-20 centimetres thick). But the Whale Shark is a harmless giant. The only danger comes when it accidentally crashes into boats or its enormous tail accidentally knocks divers! Whale Sharks are so peaceful they'll even allow divers to hold onto their fins for a ride in the ocean!

The biggest feeds on the smallest The Whale Shark feeds on some of the sea's smallest creatures. They cruise along sucking in sea water which contains tiny plants and animals called plankton. As the water passes over the gills and out through the gill-slits, the food is strained out by filters and swallowed.

Why does it feed on such small animals? Whale Sharks don't bite or chew their food! The Whale Shark has a very narrow throat which allows only fairly small items of food to be swallowed. And the teeth of the Whale Shark can't grasp very large prey - it has 3,000 match head sized teeth!

Do Whale Sharks only eat plankton? No, not always. Sometimes they'll eat schools of small fish like sardines and occasionally bigger fish like mackerel. Sometimes fish will unknowingly jump into their enormous mouths! Whale Sharks live mostly in warm water where there is a good supply of food to keep their enormous body well fed!

BASKING SHARK

The second biggest At 8-10 metres, the gentle
Basking Shark is number two in the size stakes after
the mighty Whale Shark. But it is much slimmer
and more shark-like in shape than the Whale Shark.

Basking Sharks prefer colder water and can often be
seen around Britain, cruising slowly at the surface
like they're sunbathing or 'basking' in the sun.
Really, though, they are looking for food.

The giant fishing net

The gills of the Basking Shark are like an enormous fishing net or sieve, straining out plankton or small fish from the water as the shark swims along with its mouth wide open. Rows of fine bristles called gill-rakers do the trapping of the food.

Section of a Gill-raker

No food this winter! Basking Sharks actually shed their gill-rakers during the winter! With tiny apple-pip sized teeth and little food about during the cold winter months, it's likely that Basking Sharks don't eat for many months before a new set grow in the spring. Experts wonder what Basking Sharks do during the winter - perhaps they sink to the bottom of the sea and rest!

MEGAMOUTH

The newest shark In 1976, a new, exciting and very different type of shark was discovered. It was found by chance when one became entangled in the anchor cables of a US Navy ship in the Pacific Ocean. It was named Megamouth because of its enormous 1 metre wide mouth and only a handful have been seen since!

A mouth that glows in the dark

The Megamouth's bizarre-looking mouth is full of tiny teeth and glows in the dark! Light organs around the mouth may help to attract deep-sea shrimp into its path.

WOBBEGONG

The bearded shark! This shark looks like a lump of rock! The Wobbegong lives near coral reefs and has blotchy skin markings and a fringed beard around its head which looks like seaweed. This excellent camouflage means the Wobbegong can hide from enemies.

It can also help it to catch food. As it lies on the sea-bed, the Wobbegong can suddenly grab fish, crabs or lobsters that come too close!

Dangerous or not dangerous?

The only danger comes when a diver accidentally stands on one because they're so difficult to see! The Wobbegong is also called the Carpet Shark because of its carpet-like colouring and the way it lies like a carpet on the sea-bed!

ANGEL SHARK

Run over by a steamroller! Like the Wobbegong, the harmless Angel sharks are as flat as pancakes - as if a steamroller has gone over a normal shaped shark. Angel sharks often bury themselves in the sand on the sea-bed with just their eyes on the lookout for fish!

Angels and monks Angel sharks are named after their pectoral fins which look like the wings of angels. They are also called monkfish because their heads are shaped like the hood on a monk's cloak! Angel sharks are able to breathe by drawing in water through holes on the top of their head. Some people eat Angel sharks!

FRILLED SHARK

It looks more like an eel! This odd looking shark has a long thin eel-like body, a lizard-like head and 6 gill slits (most sharks have 5) which are covered by frills - hence its name. This shark lives hundreds of metres below the surface and eats octopus, squid and fish - sometimes swallowing them whole.

GOBLIN SHARK

Back from the dead A Goblin Shark was found about 100 years ago. Until then, it was thought they had all died out 90 million years ago! The Goblin Shark is probably the ugliest shark, looking like a fantastical monster from a fairy tale with its long pointed snout. Scientists know very little about this 3 metre shark.

SAW SHARK

Saws through fish These 1-2 metre sharks have a long snout with teeth like a saw along each side! By swinging this 'saw', the shark can stun or slice through fish. It might also be used on the sea-bed for digging up shellfish or in defence.

COOKIE-CUTTER

Mystery bites! At just half a metre long, the Cookie-Cutter is a small shark but it has an interesting bite. For some time, people couldn't explain why some whales, dolphins and seals had round bites in their skin. Now we know it is the Cookie-Cutter!

The swivel bite As it bites in, the Cookie-Cutter swivels and removes an oval piece of flesh. It must be quite painful for the victim! Cookie-Cutters have even taken bites out of undersea cables and parts of submarines.

Goddess of light The scientific name for the Cookie-Cutter derives from the Egyptian goddess of light, Isis. This is because the Cookie-Cutter, like many small sharks of the deep, has light organs on its body which glow in the dark - probably to attract animals to come close enough to be bitten!

ANCIENT SHARKS

Extinct

The very first sharks to appear in the sea are now extinct but there used to be 2-3,000 different types. Some sharks living today (like the Cow and Cat sharks) are probably descended from sharks that lived 200 million years ago.

The first Great White

The most famous ancient shark is the Megalodon, the shark that all other sea creatures would have feared millions of years ago. This shark had 6 inch long teeth and jaws which were 2 metres across. The shark itself could have been over 13 metres long - double the size of today's Great White. The Megalodon or similar sized sharks could have been around as little as 12,000 years ago. Early man may have seen them!

A good fossil

A 2 metre shark called Cladoselache is one of the earliest known sharks. An excellent fossil of a Cladoselache was found in America in the 1880s. Normally it is only the hard teeth of sharks that remain, but in this case the skeleton and organs like the liver remained. Ancient fish have also been found preserved in the stomach of this shark!

Cladoselache

Stethacanthus - a prickly shark

This 1 metre shark had a big patch of teeth-like denticles on its back and head. Perhaps it used them to grip onto other fish, like remoras do today. If another animal tried to eat a Stethacanthus, it would have had a prickly surprise!

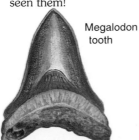

Megalodon tooth

FAMOUS SHARKS, LEGENDS AND STORIES

The most famous shark?

This is the Great White Shark that starred in Peter Benchley's 1970s film 'Jaws' which was seen by (and scared) millions of people! It was about an American seaside town terrorised by a man-eating Great White.

Respect!

Some people think sharks have special powers and have worshipped them for thousands of years. In Hawaii, a shark king called Kamo Hoa Lii is worshipped, and in New Guinea, no-one dare kill a shark for risk of offending the sea gods!

The power of sharks

Hawaiian Islanders also thought their dead relatives would come back to life as sharks. Some sailors tied shark tails to their boats to bring good luck. Solomon Islanders made shark-shaped chains hoping they

would keep sharks out of their fishing nets. On the Pacific island of Samoa, models of sharks in coconut trees were supposed to protect the fruit! Even the Romans believed in the power of sharks, rubbing children's teeth with shark brains to ease teething pain!

Using the image of sharks

During the Second World War, some American fighter planes were painted with a shark-like mouth and teeth to make them look more frightening! Australian Aborigines used to paint shark pictures on tree barks and some people think that in the biblical story, it was a shark and not a whale that swallowed Jonah.

A fishy tale

In 1799, a shark swallowed some identity papers which had been thrown overboard by the captain of a US ship. The captain didn't want the chasing British ship to discover who he was. But the shark was caught by a fisherman who found the papers inside the shark and the captain of the US ship was sent to prison!

Legless!

In 1964, Australian diver Henri Bource lost the lower part of his right leg when he was attacked by a shark. Four years later he was attacked by another shark which removed his artificial right leg!

SHARK ATTACKS

How likely am I to be attacked by a shark?

You are more likely to be struck by lightning! Each year about 30 people die from shark attacks. Compare this with the 300 people who die every year from bee-stings in America! So although sharks do kill people, just imagine all the thousands of hours spent by people in the sea all over the world for so few deaths ...

Where do most shark attacks occur?

Attacks are most common around Australia, East and South Africa, parts of North America, South Asia and Japan and the Mediterranean Sea. But shark attacks have also been recorded in colder waters and even Britain has experienced a few. In 1971, a diver was attacked by a Porbeagle Shark off the south coast of Devon.

Red area : Sharks are most common

Which sharks make the most attacks?

The Great White is the most dangerous. The Tiger, Bull, Mako, Hammerhead and Grey Reef Sharks are also known man-eaters.

Why do sharks attack people?

Not always because they're hungry! Many attacks could occur because the shark feels frightened or threatened if a swimmer or diver gets too close. Sharks may not like strangers nearby.

Mistaken identity

Most attacks probably result from the shark mistaking a person for something it normally eats. Someone lying on a surfboard with their arms outstretched looks just like a seal from underneath!

Spear fishermen are often attacked

This is because a speared fish will leave a trail of blood in the water and attract a shark. If the spearman doesn't let the shark have the fish, he may be attacked!

People don't taste very nice!

Sharks aren't normally that attracted to people - they're not used to our smell. If a shark does bite into a person, it will often let go and swim away, although sometimes leaving the victim with a horrific injury.

The unrecorded shark attacks

During the war, countless parachutists or seamen from sinking ships were probably attacked by sharks and even today, shipping disasters and plane crashes could result in attacks. But no one knows how many.

How to recognise if a shark is about to attack

Before an attack, the swimming movements of a shark become more exaggerated their snout points up, their back arches and the pectoral fins are held downwards at the side of the body. Sharks will often slowly circle many times. The circle gets smaller and smaller until the shark feels confident and then moves in.

How to avoid being attacked by a shark

Here are some simple steps: avoid murky waters where sharks could mistake you for a seal. Don't hang around in the water if there is bait or blood around, particularly if you've cut yourself and the wound is bleeding. Look out for signs on beaches which warn of sharks in the area. And don't provoke sharks - not even small ones lying on the sea-bed!

If you are ever approached by a shark, keep calm. It's probably a good idea to swim away strongly. If the shark comes too close, try punching its sensitive snout or eyes!

Nets
Nets stop sharks reaching bathers at popular beach resorts. They are made from steel or wire and are set up across the entrance to a beach. But nets are too expensive to be used at every beach and can't fully protect an area. They only last a few weeks because seaweed soon makes them easy to see and avoid by sharks.

But nets kill everything!
All types of sea life - dolphins and turtles as well as sharks - get caught in the nets and die. In Australia and Africa many hundreds of sharks are killed causing some local populations of sharks to seriously decline.

The harmless bubble option
Sometimes, hose-pipes are put on the sea-bed to release bubbles into the water. This forms a sort of bubble curtain which may discourage sharks from swimming through.

Because sharks are sensitive to electric currents, another idea is to have electric barriers across beaches which could keep sharks away without killing them.

Do beaches still have lifeguards on the look-out for sharks?
Yes, particularly in Australia. The lifeguard sounds a siren if a shark is spotted and swimmers must leave the water for however long the shark stays nearby.

What can divers do to stop an attack?

All sorts of chemicals have been used as shark
repellents but they tend to be ineffective - they
disperse easily in water. Some divers carry a long
stick which can be used to prod away any sharks.
As a last resort the diver could use his 'bangstick'.
This rod contains an explosive device which kills the
shark. In Sri Lanka, snake charmers have been tried
to keep sharks away from pearl divers!

The inflatable bag

One method of shark
protection that does
seem to work is a large
inflatable bag in which
a person stands while in
the water. Sharks can't
see or smell the person,
nor detect any electrical
impulses, and will
swim away.

STUDYING SHARKS

Is it easy to study sharks?

No! Sharks are fast moving and often live in very deep water. The best way to study the big dangerous sharks is from steel cages which are lowered into the sea. Dead fish and sometimes horse meat is put into the water to attract the sharks. Scientists sometimes have to wait days for the right species of shark to come along! Cages allow sharks to be studied and photographed very close up. Although the cage bars are strong enough and close enough together to prevent sharks biting through and attacking the diver, sharks sometimes damage the cage and knock over the diver inside with their great strength! Some scientists prefer to swim freely with sharks, particularly the less aggressive sharks like the Blue Shark.

What can be learnt from this study?

Scientists can discover the mood of the shark by watching it swim, whether it's aggressive, relaxed or curious and tell if a shark is safe to approach - some people believe that all sharks can be harmless if approached the right way.

The shark suit

Some divers study sharks while looking like knights in armour! The shark suit is made from 400,000 interlocking steel rings and prevents the shark from biting through a diver's limbs. Divers can even hand-feed sharks while wearing this suit, although it is rather heavy and difficult to swim in.

Tagging sharks

This is when a small piece of metal is attached to the shark's dorsal fin. When the shark is next caught, scientists can tell how much the shark has grown. Thousands of sharks have been tagged over the last few decades and one Australian Tope was caught 35 years after it was tagged!

Radio sharks

Sometimes a more sophisticated tag is used which gives off radio signals. This allows scientists to follow the shark wherever it goes and find out how fast and how far it swims.

Enemies of sharks

Because of their size and speed, sharks have few enemies. Killer Whales will sometimes attack sharks and so will dolphins - to protect their young they ram the shark's gills with their snouts! And sharks will often kill each other. They can live for 60 years, perhaps even 70-100 years. But to live that long they have to avoid their greatest enemy - man.

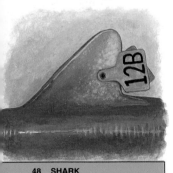